SMACK ON THIS

Veronica J.

Contents

Dedication

This work is dedicated to my Grandfather, Rev. Mills C. Cooper, and my grandmother (Bigmamma) Clementine Roberson Cooper, who founded and Pastored several Baptist churches throughout Georgia and Florida. To my parents, Deacon Eddie Louis and Mother Maggie McKenzie. Thank you all for laying the foundation and assuring me that I know the way to righteousness. To my sisters Glo and Mae! Everyone should have sisters like my sisters. You believed in me when I did not believe in myself.

Acknowledgment

There are a number of persons who helped to inspire this labor of love project. I am thankful for my family members, cousins, and my two remaining uncles, who are pillars of strength and courage for me, Carlton Cooper and Eddie Cooper. Your presence inspires me. You preached my soul out of hell to my adopted spiritual Mom & Pops, Superintendent Charles, and Mother Lottie Lewis. To my daughter and little cousin, Telisha and Courtney. You two pushed me! To the only wise God, my Savior, be all the glory!

About the Author

Veronica Elaine Jones was born and raised in Pasco County, Florida. She is the youngest of six siblings. She is married to David, a retired law enforcement officer and graduate of Howard University. Their blended family consists of four boys and two girls, all adults and, she is a proud grandmother.

Her 28 years in legal services and her work as a Community Outreach Coordinator with Bay Area Legal Services helped guide her passion and commitment to social justice. Elaine has a B.A. in Education and Public Policy, an M.A. in Teaching and Learning with Technology. She is currently pursuing a Ph.D. in Education with a concentration in Racial Justice and Access to Legal Services. Elaine is passionate about the word of God and is licensed with her Church, where she teaches, instructs, and conducts inspirational workshops and messages. Finally, she is the creator of her brand "Lucid Smack," a brand geared towards providing clear and understandable truths to strengthen and empower the lives of those she touches.

Interesting Facts:

A sense of self-worth grounds her.

Her mantra for moving forward; educate to remain relevant.

Preface

This book is a collection of awe-inspiring messages and topics under the direct unction of the Lord through the prophet and is the first in a series. The reader is provoked to follow along with their bible in hand. The author encourages your feedback. Prepare to be challenged.

Chapter 1:
Signs of the End

How much trust should one put in a sign? Do signs have any worth when it comes to the quality of life and living that one experiences? Are there any signs that are affecting the quality of your life? Smack on this!

The Bible speaks of the many signs we will see in this world concerning world status, past, present, and future. The Lord God has created a system of communication through signs to help guide all who seek to know and love him to live their best lives. Based upon our degree of knowledge of God's Word, we have a degree of discernment of the signs of approval or warning and guidance required for a spiritual existence.

Our actions, reactions, and quality of life directly correlate to a spiritual connection to God, who desires us to live sinless lives. Based upon biblical beliefs, we will suffer in this world and the afterlife if we choose to ignore and minimize biblical standards.

What Are the Signs?

The dictionary definition of 'sign' is *"a mark having customary/conventional/ ordinary meaning, used in place of words to represent a complex notion."*

It indicates or expresses the existence of something not immediately apparent. It hints towards an event that is about to happen. The Hebrew understanding of this word is; 'an outward token having spiritual significance.' Further, the Greek meaning of the word means 'a signal, i.e., flag, beacon, monument, omen, prodigy, evidence, mark.'

There are several mentions of 'signs' in the Bible. One common example is found in Genesis 9:12-17. It touches upon a sign indicative of the covenant/promise God made with man; he would never destroy the world with water again and ensured the covenant between God and his creation. As God said to the prophet Noah, "This is the sign of the covenant I have established between me and all life on the earth." Genesis is known as the book of beginnings. We understand that *the bow (a divine sign)* was set to remind us what would be and is yet to come. No water will ever destroy the earth again. Instead, there will be an unquenchable fire.

Purpose of Biblical Signs

God has given signs for many purposes. A few of the vital ones are outlined here:

Authenticate a prophecy: In Deuteronomy 13, prophet Moses declares that if a prophet gives a sign that asks you to worship other gods, then that prophet shall be put to death because he has spoken to turn you away from the Lord.

And in Luke 12:2, Angels appeared to the shepherds in the field, proclaiming the fulfillment of the prophecy of baby Jesus. When they declared, "This shall be a sign unto you, you shall find the babe wrapped in swaddling clothes."

Strengthen Your Faith: In Judges 6:37, Gideon needed to strengthen his faith when praying to the Lord. So he asked God in no uncertain terms if He would be there, let the fleece be wet, and the ground all around it be dry. God then showed him a sign that He would be there.

Now, let's discuss the primary scriptures pointing towards the signs we will see during our lifetimes. These signs are put in place to help indicate our spiritual location and remind us of God-given time constraints and restraints as we near the end of all things as we know them.

Perilous/Difficult times Shall Come: The hardships and difficulties that we are experiencing reflect God's word predicted. Relatedly, there was a time when, if you were not interested in religion and the Church, you simply stayed away. But the more complex our world becomes, there are those infiltrating the Church who seek to hold positions and offices but never seek to know God and are unrepentant for their wrongdoing. Furthermore, the truth of God's word is being dangerously mixed with political rhetoric, as millions are misled by this toxic exploitation of God's word.

Individuals seek to affiliate and make allegiance with the Church and its members, who have either not received or believe in the gift of the Holy Ghost. The Holy Ghost is an empowering and indwelling of strength, given by God, to commission a sustainable Christian life. Furthermore, some individuals claim Christ, yet deny the power of the Holy Ghost, and are corrupt in their deeds. An evil spirit controls and causes people to lie, cheat and do whatever it takes to get the job done, with no concern for ethics or Christ-like morals.

Such people are all around us. Kindness and affableness have been replaced with arrogance and lies. It then becomes the duty of authentic and faithful Christians to warn, sound the alarm, and inform that spiritual adjustment needs to be made if you believe in the afterlife and, ultimately, if you believe in the Word of God. Considering the climate of current times, we must maintain a steady and consistent posture of faith and adherence to biblical principles. If we believe in God's Word, we must live like it!

Times are dangerous, challenging, and perilous, and these all serve as signs. There is a continued fight against corruption and abhorrence towards other faiths. Two traitors inside the Church can be far more dangerous than 200,000 men outside the church. These types of actions cause significant disruptions and is why the Church is in such TURMOIL – and this is just a sign.

Lovers of Their Own Selves – SELF-LOVE: Men who love their carnal selves more than their spiritual lives are also signs. In this Day and age, humans love their own gratification more than church edification – putting their own agenda before anything that pertains to God. We are in the midst of a 'selfie' nation and world.

People do not consider the House of God as a sacred sanctuary. Preaching God's word has to do with improving your spiritual connection with God by adopting biblical principles. Instead, ministers give classes on saving up riches and becoming millionaires. There is advice on retiring rich, and none of the scriptures are taught adequately because of a thirst and lust for filthy lucre.

In place of strengthening God's Word within his people, there is a desire to renovate buildings to be bigger and grander than the rest. So the Lord speaks in Matthew 6:33, "But seek ye first the Kingdom of God AND His righteousness."

Covetous: Again, we find SELF-LOVE at the root of covetousness. Many people are promising you that, "I'll come to help you with your issue because that will help me GET MY NAME OUT THERE" or saying something along the lines of, "I have got to get something out of this deal."

This is a dangerous mindset to live with. The attitude of covetousness is not exclusively connected to church activities but can be found in people's everyday lives, where people are not diligently helping people. Instead, such individuals desire worldly benefits such as money and fame (tangible goods that lead to intangible disasters).

The Bible declares in Timothy 6:10, "For the love of money is the root of all evil." This shows that obsessing over materialistic goods will eventually destroy you. Not caring for your brother's welfare makes a man dangerous/difficult, and it's JUST A SIGN.

Boasting and Being Proud: There is no wrong in being confident in your faith, yet God's Word is clear that he hates a proud look. Soloman speaks of this in the book of Proverbs 6:16-17, six things that the Lord hates, and is even an abomination to him, "a proud look." Society and the

Churches have developed habits of despising and looking down on others because they have not, will not, or cannot accomplish highly coveted and worldly accomplishments.

Honor and respect for others are becoming more rarely seen among churchgoers, which indicates a turning away and disrespect for the only true and living God. When a man does not fear God, he will not regard men, as seen throughout the Church and everyday life. Instead, people have become full of themselves, bragging and feeling superior when their achievements are better than others.

The Bible declares in Proverbs 16:18 that "Pride goes before destruction, a haughty spirit before a fall." And it's JUST A SIGN

Disobedient to Parents: Are you old enough to see how the role of children has changed towards parents and guardians? There was a time when parents and guardians led the way of righteousness and Godly living. Modern-day standards have seen a role reversal, wherein children determine their direction of faith without regard to parental guidance. Such behavior gives way for role reversal and disobedience to the scriptures, as Proverbs 22:6 instructs, "Train up a child in the way he should go: and when he is old, he will not depart from it." As a result, they have lost their God-given authority.

Biblical principles require children to surrender and embrace their parents/parental figures. Guardians, parents, and parental figures, please take your God-given places. Unfortunately, this fundamental concept seems to have gone out the window.

Newsflash: You will always be your parents' child. They brought you up and took care of your needs, which is why disobedience to the very people who brought you into this world and nurtured you is JUST A SIGN.

Unthankful and Unholy: There exists a generation in which gratitude and thankfulness are a scarcity. Further, the climate of current times refuses to be pleased, brought on by a spirit of unholiness. In the book of Leviticus, 6:10, the Bible instructs that there is a difference between holy and not holy and further requires that we put differences in places where there are none. And thankful hearts are mandated in scripture, as I Thessalonians 5:18 urges, "In everything give thanks, for this is the will of God in Christ Jesus concerning you."

God's Word is clear that we must maintain a degree of separation of the things which are clean and set apart for God from those things which are not. Therefore, those who have chosen God as their Lord and Savior should not find themselves locked into such activities as smoking, excessive drinking (*total abstinence*), cursing, and disrespecting those in authority.

Seeking worldly pleasures and goods renders the church body powerless for the manifestation of a sincere move of God. Authentic worship must proceed from genuine hearts. The writer, John in 4:24, declares, "God is a spirit: and they that worship him must worship him in spirit and in truth."

God said to Moses in Leviticus 10:3, "I will be sanctified in them that come near me, and before all the people I will be glorified." But, unfortunately, there seems to be a lapse in memory concerning this portion of the Lord's words.

The Word of the Lord from Exodus 3:5 says, "Do not draw near this place. Take your sandals off your feet, for the place where you stand is holy ground." There is no reverence for the House of the ONLY TRUE AND LIVING GOD, so our recklessness towards God's Church is JUST A SIGN.

Without Natural Affection: We live in a time when men will not hold to the demands of nature. Men have changed their sexual orientation, and women have transformed themselves to look more like men.

Men and women are coming forward to declare that they have always liked the same gender and that they were born this way. So the good news is that you can be BORN again, and this too is JUST A SIGN.

Trucebreakers – People of today are oath breakers. No conscience of the engagements or commitments that they have made. "Do you promise to uphold and defend the rules of the Holy Writ, priesthood, church, laws, and standards?" they are asked, and they affirm 'yes.' Then they soon turn and disrespect leaders and authorities, and ultimately the Lord. This is all JUST A SIGN.

False Accusers – There is little regard for the good name of others. It seems that no *name* is sacred, whether it be the President, Pastor, or the Priestly name of our Lord and Savior, Jesus Christ. It is acceptable these days to have the liberty to say what you want about whomever you want, whenever you want. It's JUST A SIGN.

Incontinent & Fierce – No Self Control: These are the days when men will not govern themselves or their appetites. Christians today don't fast as they used to, even though it is emphasized in God's Word. Caution must be taken, that there always remains a command over our own spirits. Care must be taken to ward against attitudes that convey a "Nobody tells me what to say" position. Efforts must be put forth to comply with the teachings of God's Word. As Psalms 12:4 says, "With our tongue will we prevail; our lips are our own: who is LORD over us?".

We must be careful to ensure that we look not upon what is good for us with contempt and disdain because this will cause us to go astray from God's Word. Man has become treacherous, willful, and arrogant. It's JUST A SIGN.

Traitors and High-Minded:

"Brother will betray brother to death, and a father his child; children will rebel against their parents and have them put to death" – (Matthew 10:21)

Nowadays, it is common for those who confess Christ to be unfaithful to each other to get their way with things. There are common occurrences where the climate within houses of worship is designed as entertainment stages. Men and women are praised for their gifts and talents, which is not altogether inaccurate, yet the true purpose of the gifts is to glorify God and bring the message of God to the masses. Church ministries must guard against promoting an atmosphere that only serves selfish and insincere desires and motives. Seek humility and encourage it. James 4:10 reads, "Humble yourselves in the sight of the Lord, and he shall lift you up." It is a misfortune, but we also have church people who are irritable and peevish, always cross or complaining, moody, fretful, and irritable. It's JUST A SIGN.

Lovers of Pleasure More Than Lovers of God: There are more Epicureans in the Church than Christians. In other words, there are more philosophers – social sophisticates – with a sensitive and unique taste in food and wines but no desire for the sincere milk of the Word of God. As the Lord, through 1Peter 2:1-2 instructs, "Wherefore laying aside all malice, and all guile, and hypocrisies, and envies, and all evil speakings, as newborn babes, desire the sincere milk of the word, that you may grow thereby. They are inclined more towards finding satisfaction in this world rather than spiritual enrichment for the world to come. It's JUST A SIGN.

Having a form of Godliness but Denying the Power Thereof: There are sects within Christendom who are called by Christ's name, baptized in His name, sing so melodiously for Him. Yet they preach with no conviction or Power of the Holy Ghost.

So with ALL THESE SIGNS, He promises that those who shall endure and hold out until the end shall be SAVED. The work presented here is meant to help shed a clearer understanding of the pertinence of the events and happenings before the world ends. Allow these words to stir your pure minds as a reminder that we are living in the END TIMES. God is calling for repentance.

He's coming soon.

He is angry. He loves you. It is incumbent upon you to prepare now. Today! There is no tomorrow for those who die today.

Chapter 2:
Heaven Yes,
But Hell?

Hell is more than a curse word. It is a physical location. The following offers a scripture depiction about Hell, a final destination. This will be a reminder for some. Others, we pray, will be informed of a place called Hell. The Bible speaks of no such place as purgatory. Even though, according to Webster's dictionary, the word purgatory is defined as an intermediate state after death in which souls are purified after death or a state of temporary punishment. Unfortunately, contrary to popular belief, there is no purgatory, only the choice between HEAVEN and HELL. Smack on this!

If there was a choice of a final resting place, which would you choose, Heaven or Hell? The obvious choice for most would be Heaven, right? But Hell?... 'NO'.

The Real Place After Death

Hell is a real place where many will spend eternity after death, and they will be banned from the Lord's presence forever. The death that we will die in this world is only a repository. Once death has dealt its blow, then souls are required to hold on until that GREAT JUDGMENT DAY, when we will be awakened for placement into heaven, or hell, according to the deeds done in our body's lifetime.

There's an old adage that declares, "When you're dead, you're done." Unfortunately, it is not entirely true because while no more can be done on this side, there is still the Judgment on the other side of this life.

"It is appointed unto man once to die, but after this the judgment." – (Hebrew 9:27).

My granddaddy died over 30 years ago. Moses and the prophets left centuries and decades ago. But no matter how decayed the corpse or how dried the bones, the Lord will order all to get up during the Day of judgment. The Word of the Lord declares that the dead shall rise first.

"Write, for these words are true and faithful." - (Revelation 21:5)

What Is Hell Like?

The standard description of Hell is that of FIRE. But it goes beyond just that.

Hell is not just FIRE, but it is FLAMES OF FIRE.

"For, behold, the Lord will come with fire, and with his chariots like a whirlwind, to render his anger with fury, and his rebuke with flames of fire."
– (Isaiah 66:15)

Hell is a FURNACE OF FIRE

"The Son of Man will send out his angels, and they will weed out of his kingdom everything that causes sin and all who do evil. They will throw them into the blazing furnace, where there will be weeping and gnashing of teeth."

— (Matthew 13:41-42)

Hell's Fire is UNQUENCHABLE

"And if your eye causes you to stumble, pluck it out. It is better for you to enter the kingdom of God with one eye than to have two eyes and be thrown into Hell fire: Where their worm dieth not, and the fire is not quenched."

— (Mark 9:47-48)

In other words, you can try to stop it, roll in it, or try to ease the pain in any way, but the fire refuses and is incapable of being put out.

Hell is DARK

"And throw that worthless servant outside, into the darkness, where there will be weeping and gnashing of teeth."

— (Matthew 25:30)

Hell Has WIND

"On the wicked, He will rain down fiery coals and sulfur; a scorching wind will be their portion."

— (Psalm 11:6)

Hell STINKS

"But the fearful, and unbelieving, and the abominable, and murderers, and whoremongers, and sorcerers, and idolaters, and all liars, shall have their part in the lake which burneth with fire and brimstone: which is the second death."

– (Revelation 21:8)

Brimstone (sulfur) is found primarily in hot springs and volcanic craters. It has a distinct rotten egg smell caused by sulfur dioxide gases released in the air. In other words, Hell is not just hot and dark, but it stinks terribly like rotten eggs.

Hell Has UNDYING WORMS

Dead bodies are known for having worms that feed on decaying flesh until it's gone, and then the worms die. But as Jesus warns, *"The worms that eat them do not die, and the fire is not quenched."*

– (Mark 9:48)

You ask me if I want to go to Heaven' YES' but HELL…

Hell's fire is ETERNAL.

"If your hand or your foot causes you to stumble, cut it off and throw it away. It is better for you to enter life maimed or crippled than to have two hands or two feet and be thrown into eternal fire."

– (Matthew 18:8)

Hell is ALWAYS SMOKEY, and it NEVER RESTS

It says clearly in Revelation 14:10-11 that, *"They will be tormented with burning sulfur in the presence of the holy angels and of the Lamb. And the smoke of their torment will rise forever and ever."*

Hell is a LAKE OF FIRE

"And the beast was taken, and with him the false prophet that wrought miracles before him, with which he deceived them that had received the mark of the beast, and them that worshipped his image. These both were cast alive into a lake of fire burning with brimstone."

– (Revelation 19:20)

What Is Hell's Purpose?

Hell was prepared for the devil and his angels. Matthew 25:41 says, "Then He will say to those on His left, 'Depart from Me, you who are cursed, into the eternal fire prepared for the devil and his angels." But in Isaiah 5:14, the Bible informs that, "Hell has ENLARGED herself and opened her mouth without measure."

In other words, Hell is a crowded place. Matthew 7:13 says: "…for wide is the gate and broad is the way that leads to destruction, and many there be that go in that way."

Hell's Myth

There are some things to bear in mind: On the great judgment day, the entire world will be summoned by God from the beginning of time. The young and old from every corner of the Earth, including the likes of Adolph Hitler, Charles Manson, all the suicide bombers, and every other sinful human, will be summoned.

Many people laugh off their sins by saying that Hell will be like one big party. Yet, considering what we have reviewed thus far, it doesn't sound like much of a party.

The question is, "do you want to go to heaven? Yes. But hell? No.

This Is for The Young People

Do babies and children go to Hell? The Lord does not discriminate when He says in Ezekiel 18:4, "Behold, every soul belongs to Me; both father and son are Mine. The soul who sins is the one who will die."

Psalm 51:5 also states, "Behold I was shaped in iniquity, and in sin did my mother conceive me."

God understands and knows all and can judge the sins of babies and children on their level of understanding. Paul declares in Hebrews. 4:12b that the Word of God is a discerner of the thoughts and intents of the heart. He even knows your thoughts before you even think them.

So children should be taught the right way from the start to protect them from the fire on judgment day. God knows everything, and He does not forgive everyone.

"Train up a child in the way he should go" – (Proverbs. 22:6)

Is Your Name On Hell's Roll Call?

Do you think that you have led a sinful life? What are your sins? The Bible mentions the acts that are frowned upon by God, and if you are one of those persons who commit those acts, it is time to rethink your choices in life.

"People will be lovers of themselves, lovers of money, boastful, proud, abusive, disobedient to their parents, ungrateful, unholy, without love, unforgiving, slanderous, without self-control, brutal, not lovers of the good, treacherous, rash, conceited, lovers of pleasure rather than lovers of God— having a form of godliness but denying its Power. Have nothing to do with such people."

- (Timothy 3:2-5)

Other sins are mentioned in the Bible, including blasphemers, without natural affection, trucebreakers, false accusers, incontinent, fierce, high-minded, cheaters, prostitutes, and lovers of pleasure more than lovers of God. The list goes on to include greed for filthy lucre, drunkards, swindlers, impure (*none but the pure in heart*), witchcraft, discord, jealously, envy, lying, cowardice, unbelieving, sexual immorality, hatred/hateful, murders.

Love Break

God created us to have a loving relationship with Him. We were created for His glory, but man rebelled and sinned at the 'fall' from Heaven. But God has a love potion to bring humans back on track.

"For God so loved the world that he gave his one and only Son, that whoever believes in him shall not perish but have eternal life."

– **(John 3:16)**

The Wrap Up

Hell exists for the requital and retribution of evil deeds. In other words, we are thrown into the pits of fire as a way to pay for our sins. It is the place of final judgment and the point of "No Return." Once you get there, there is NO WAY OUT.

This brings to mind the story of the rich man and Lazarus in the Bible. The moral of the story is that poor godly people – the ones whom men reject and ridicule, ignore, and trample on, maybe mistreated, but there is a God who keeps tally on all deeds, actions, and behaviors that must be accounted for in the end.

God's Word warns that Christians are counted as sheep for the slaughter and are often mean and miserably treated. For this reason, we are required to keep the focus on the goal, eternal life, no matter how difficult it may become at times. One moment living in God's kingdom will pay for all of the hardships and mistreatment encountered during this earthly existence.

The rich man lost his mind in Hell, saying anything to get out of there in the story. He has enough cognizance to recognize Lazarus, the poor beggar that was constantly at his gate begging, while they were both on this side of eternity. This rich man had total disdain for the poor beggar and refused to give him any type of relief or comfort. This is for certain; God has a way of bringing the events and deeds of our lives to full circle. In this parable, the rich man said he would take a drop of water from the "sore infested" beggar. He was willing to do anything to receive the slightest bit of comfort or relief. He petitioned the Lord to allow him to return as a dead man; he would even preach as a dead man!

And if we could ask him right now, I believe he would say to us, Heaven? Yes! But, Hell? No!

In conclusion, Hell is a place designed by God to separate those who love Him from those who hate Him. Therefore, the Lord urges, "If you love me, keep my commands." And we must start saving up on our good deeds and dismissing our sinful acts, or else it will be too late.

The Day is coming when God shall separate the good from the bad, the wicked from the Godly. The rich and the poor will not be separated, nor will the educated and uneducated be kept differently. Only the Godly will be on the right and the Ungodly on the left. All other divisions and subdivisions will be abolished! There will be no Bishop Heaven and Missionary Hell but a final division of Saints and Sinners, the Sanctified and Unsanctified.

It is at times painfully evident that we dwell together, in the same cities, in the same families, with those who refuse to believe and those who are abhorrent to the truth of the only true and living God. And there are times when it is laborious to distinguish between the believer and the unbeliever.

But on that Great Judgment Day, we will be separated FOREVER!

From the sullenest and quietest sinner, snuggled up among the saints, to the most philanthropic sinner, no one will be able to confuse or refute God's Judgment. Furthermore, it would bring great comfort on this side of heaven to know that the life lived here on earth, and the deed done in this body, would prompt the Lord to pronounce these promised words, "Come, ye blessed of the Father" (Matt. 25:34).

There is an old negro spiritual entitled "What do you want the Lord to say?" If you want Him to welcome you into eternal Glory, then you must amend and align your way to that of his world. It is imperative that we understand that the end is coming, and we must make sure that we are ready at his return without a shadow of a doubt.

The Lord has prepared a place. He designed it from the foundation of the world. The end comes last, executing the proper closure to our doings in this world. So He is coming, even if we are ready or not. Heaven? Yes. But, Hell? No!